Sam
On The
Way

ISBN: 978-0-6151-8759-4

Dear ?,

Nine months is a long time to wait for something you really want. You will be here any day now and we are excited, anxious, and nervous. Above all, we love you and always will.

Dad

December 9, 2006

Introduction

It's amazing what you can re-learn from a child, or about yourself when you're expecting a child. Smiling is better than frowning. Giving is better than receiving. There are more important things to do than check your email – like laugh so hard you can't stand up.

This isn't a book of lessons though, as I can't really claim to be a great teacher. It's certainly not a how-to parenting book, as I'm really just getting started as a parent and winging most of it. These are just a collection of letters to my son, mostly *for* my son.

This collection started out as one letter when my wife and I found out we had a baby on the way – in April of 2006. It grew into this collection, each letter re-affirming that I had no idea what was in store for me as a Father. Really, I was just starting to figure out what it meant to be an adult.

We live in Atlanta, Georgia just north of the heart of the city. The south has been home to my wife for basically her entire life and it's been home to me for almost half of mine. This means of course, that I would still be a Yankee on any given UGA game day in Athens.

Truthfully, I won't claim to be a legit Southerner since I'm still not on the same page with my wife's family when it comes to syllable management: I think my wife's name is *one* syllable and mine is *two*. But when it's fixin' to be dinner time, "Jee-ill" (two syllables) and "Brine" (one syllable) get called to the table by her family.

This book is dedicated to Sam ("Saah-am") who provided both the material and the inspiration. Perhaps you will relate to the pregnancy stories or perhaps you will relate to the bumbling father stories. The letters are not all happy-go-lucky, but they are all real. And the letters are complete with all their non-edited, screwy-grammar glory...so please overlook what I should've learned in 9th grade English.

Perhaps you are considering starting a family or perhaps you'd just like to follow along for the ride. No matter what the reason, thank you and enjoy my letters to Sam.

Found Out!

Tuesday April 18, 2006

Dear Donnie and Marie:

Your Mom is a terrible poker player. I knew within the first few words when she called me at the office today and in the way her voice was charged with excitement that she had good news.

"Good morning" I answered the phone.

"Hey, it's me," your Mom said in a nervous, I-may-have-won-the-lottery voice.

"Heeyyyyy," I musically dragged out my response, wondering what the news was.

"I think I'm pregnant," she blurted out.

"Yaaahhhhh!" I cheered.

You see, (Young-Mr.-or-Ms.-whatever-we-end-up-naming-you) about a month ago we were hoping that this might happen, and that nine months later we would get to meet you.

Jill wasn't feeling too well this morning and decided to take one of the home pregnancy tests she bought in bulk and stock-piled after we decided to try to get pregnant. Then she took another test, and another, and another. And something made her feel comfortable enough (after the fourth positive test) to call me and tell me the wonderful news.

Later she told me the elaborate plans she had cooked-up to tell me the news – which all went out the window once she had a "real" fourth positive pregnancy test. She planned to set the table for dinner and ask me to get the rolls out of the oven – which she would purposely not turn on. I would (predictably) bark, "what is this?" And she would giggle and say "it's a bun in the oven!" Of course she has the patience of a flea with fleas, so the instant after the fourth positive test, she called me and scrapped the bun-in-the-oven shenanigan. By the way, I spend more time than I should wondering if I should use "tom foolery" or "shenanigan." I think the word shenanigan is Irish and means something involving a fox, so we'll go with that.

Anyway, I'm glad she did toss out her big BITO (bun in the oven) plan, since I was immediately all smiles. It really didn't matter that my job was being eliminated by some blind hypocritical bureaucrats or that I could barely stomach some of the dysfunctional, passive aggressive, character assassins that I worked with. On this particular day, thanks to that particular phone call, I would be all smiles in my day of meetings to put together planning committees to plan future meetings. Whoa, I digress...

I was all smiles. I hadn't really thought about a reaction to my wife being pregnant. I had seen plenty of movie-style reactions: terror, joy, pride, anger. I was just smiling. It felt good.

I knew there would be plenty of preparation ahead, a lot of assembly required, baby-proofing and a lot to learn (or pretend to learn). I'm sure I'll get agitated by a new round of showers and parties. I'm sure I'll get nervous and confused by a new world of babies. In the past, I've been that guy who thinks babies are cute, but never really felt the need to snuggle with their burp-up or full diapers.

However, I'm also sure of something else: I'm positively sure that we already love you and that we are so exited to meet and hold you that we feel like we'll explode.

This is the first letter I will write you, one of many I hope. Really, I wish you could write back, my recollection inside the womb when I was your age is a little hazy. You could tell me what's going on, what you like to eat, music you want to hear, or anything else that's on your mind. I promised your Mom I wouldn't tackle her for the next nine or so months, so you won't experience any major earth quakes.

Stay well, grow strong, hiccough and kick when you can. I love you.

Dad

Sonogram

Monday, May 15, 2006

Dear Donnie and Marie:

You may never think "Donnie and Marie" is funny, but that's what we are calling you for now. I bet most expecting parents have some name they call their little belly baby. "Parasite" was the meanest one I've heard, but we have both a better sense of humor than that mean Mom and are somewhat confident that you and your Mom are the same species.

Truth is that we, your parents, are even too young to remember much of the singing fraternal twins Donnie & Marie who made a bunch of albums in the 1970s and I actually can't name one of their tunes.

But since we won't find out if you are a boy or a girl, and I think it's funny, we'll call you Donnie and Marie until you are born. Maybe if you misbehave we'll call you that after you are born!

You are only one baby – we saw for the first time today. Just because you are one baby doesn't mean it's any less funny to call you Donnie *and* Marie.

Your Mom went in for her first sonogram today. Best way I can describe your first picture is like a charcoal sketch of a lizard after it went through the washer. No matter how bad your first school pictures will be as a teenager, they'll top this!

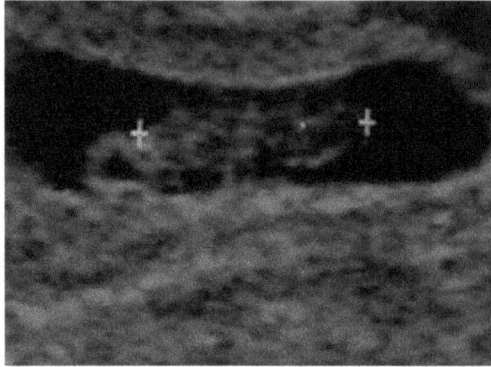

Smiling seems to be an early theme in these letters and today was no exception. I didn't go with your Mom to the doctor's appointment, I had a meeting to try and get a new job. Jobs with an expecting wife = a good thing. No job = no good.

Jill called me on my way to the meeting and said everything looked good with the sonogram. I had a goofy grin when I met with the Managing Director of a world-wide PR agency. I just told him the truth that I got the good news about my first baby. My choices were to appear wildly distracted and high on drugs or high on life because my wife is pregnant. He was delighted and congratulated me, so turned out to be a good meeting.

Now that I have my first picture of you, I can relate to those proud mothers and fathers who say "hey look at mah kid."

Being a geek is not a "yes-or-no" thing. It is a continuum. For example, I don't play video games in online chat rooms and never created cyber names in virtual worlds. I do however have a website and your first picture is now proudly displayed. So I can be my own version of a geek and email friends/family and write "hey click here and look at mah kid!"

I can't wait for more pictures to share and brag about you!

Love,

Dad

Father's Day

Thursday June 15, 2006

Dear D&M:

I celebrated my first Father's Day today, a few days early. As you will figure out eventually, I'm not that big into receiving gifts – it generally makes me feel uncomfortable, probably from celebrations growing up that were simple.

One Christmas growing up I asked for black olives – the pitted kind so I could stick them on my fingers and eat them. That's low budget. Could be that it runs in the family and I take after your Grandfather, who legitimately asks and wants things like wood glue for holiday gifts.

Your Great Aunt Carolyn, on the other hand is very, very generous and loves to celebrate. So, she wanted to take me out for "tea" to celebrate Father's Day. The "tea" stems from when your Mother went to celebrate Mother's Day a month ago. They got all girled-up with their fancy pants and had tea at the Swan House in Atlanta.

Thankfully your Great Aunt knows that actually going for tea would be excruciating pain, so she didn't take me to the Swan House.

Another thing you'll stumble on eventually is that your Mother is terrible at keeping secrets. When she asked me if I knew where your

Great Aunt was taking me for tea, I immediately had confirmation that it was not going to be the Swan House.

"Fat Matt's Rib Shack," I replied.

"Uhh, no… why would you think that?" she stumbled over, confirming that I was right.

Fat Matt's Rib Shack is really where I would like to go for tea. Sweet tea, to wash down a pile of ribs and chicken, some of which will actually make it in my mouth and not all over my clothes.

Now, this seemingly astute guess-work only mixed things up a little bit. Your Mom told Carolyn that I guess right, which just made her change venues – surprises are all part of the game.

I had thought about going into the office, on one of my last days before my job officially went away thanks to some budget cuts. But when I woke up, I just took another personal day. I had 180+ hours of sick time, with no possible way to use it all. So Carolyn picked me up for our lunch "tea" to celebrate… well, to celebrate *you* really.

A few minutes later we parked at Capital Grill steakhouse. Perfect – I usually don't put your Mom the vegetarian through such anguish, but I sho' do love me some steak.

Chowed some wonderful steak – although I really had thought we were going to Fat Matt's, so if I had known, I would've shaved and probably dressed a bit nicer.

Then we talked about you, whoever you are and will be. It was fun to imagine. Not that I have high hopes or unrealistic expectations. I certainly wouldn't wish anything like the Presidency of the United States on you. Simple, healthy, satisfied kid would be a wish-come-true.

The opportunity to pursue happiness (jeez I just caught myself sounding like the Declaration of Independence) and bounce back from inevitable failures would be ideal. I'm sure there will be Father's Days coming up that will be fun and filled with laughter, but this will always be the first one. Thanks to you and your Great Aunt Carolyn.

Love,

Dad

Paralyzing Fear

Thursday July 19, 2006

Dear Donnie and Marie:

You are in trouble – and you made me cry – and I don't mean tears of joy, but tears of a brand new kind of fear. I do NOT appreciate the paralyzing fear you just put me through and you are officially grounded for the next week. No TV, no parties, no phone calls or instant messaging or whatever else you're doing in there.

For the next week, you just sit there quietly and grow.

On July 14 (last Friday) your little tom foolery started with a routine screening – just to make sure you are OK. These are the kinds of tests that will indicate life-threatening diseases or possible abnormalities, or syndromes or any other worst of words that people use every day and mean significantly more when you are talking about the life of your child.

Your test came up positive, which is bad.

Down syndrome is something many people are familiar with, and results when an extra chromosome ends up on the 21st set. You should have two, but Down syndrome people have three. Edward's syndrome is when the same non-genetic chromosome abnormality happens, but instead of on #21, it happens on #18. The results of the screening test we got told us that you had Trisomy 18 (Edward's Syndrome), which is fatal for the baby.

In the very rare case that you were born, there would be only a 10% chance that you would survive a year before dying. The worst weekend I can remember followed the news.

I never would have guessed the way I reacted. I cried more than once. I started thinking about the words to inform friends and family that we had lost you. Then on Monday, July 17, we went in for the follow-up tests. The possibility that kept us going was the hope for a false positive, meaning the first test was wrong.

Your Mom and I went in the Doctor's office together and had an amazing ultrasound. You were kicking around, showing us some dance moves, generally enjoying yourself. No apparent deformities – your hands looked good, your size/weight were right where they were supposed to be, no obvious signs of Edward's Syndrome. But we wouldn't know for sure unless we had an amniocentesis. Your Mom, incidentally was much stronger than I was during all this – a "pillar of strength" (as I was sobbing in the Doctor's office).

We had the amnio which was pretty freaky, not to mention a 1-in-300 chance of generating a miscarriage. We watched the needle go in on one end and saw it show up on the ultrasound – with you just kind of hanging out wondering what the hell was coming in to your little protected space. We took a deep breath and left the Doctor's office.

As if that wasn't enough fun, your Mom collapsed on the way to the car, just crumpled as I tried to catch her – which just ended up being buffering her on the way to the ground.

I ran back to the Doctor's office and got the Doctor, while a complete stranger sat with your Mom. That stranger was the kind of guy who I need to buy a drink for, but I was entirely too frazzled to even get his name to say a proper thank you.

Perhaps I will get to say thanks some day, but in the mean time, I'll try to make it up for someone else in the grand karma scheme of things.

We made it back to the Doctor's office to relax. Apparently, feinting is not all the uncommon after an amnio – information that would've been better delivered on the front-end of the process.

Wednesday, July 18 was yesterday. We got the news that you had orchestrated your first prank – it was a false positive and you are as normal as you could possibly be, given who your parents are. So, you are grounded. Don't even think about doing anything like this again, we love you too much.

Just one of those things that parents go through quite a bit and get all worked-up about. Now I know why.

Dad

Kick for Dad?

Wednesday June 21, 2006

Dear Donnie and Marie:

Still no kicking from you, although you are making your Mom (what I affectionately like to call) "bust out of her pants."

Something else you are doing, which if you continue you might be getting a punishment, is flood your Mom with hormones. Cut her some slack will you? As fun as it is to come home from work to a wife stressed-out with mood swings…. laughing and crying at the same time…how 'bout giving it a break for a while?

However, I do appreciate the guidance you've given her to start nesting. It's awesome that she is going on cleaning kicks – getting rid of the stuff that she's been pack-ratting for years – like abstract magazine articles and miscellaneous garbage.

We found out today that your future play-friend and neighbor is a girl. You'll find out soon that we have absolutely awesome neighbors, the Weiners (pronounced "Weener").

Your future playmate will be born in October/November, so you will have a girlfriend just a few months older waiting for you in December!

Love,
Dad

Soccer Player

Monday August 28, 2006

Dear Donnie and Marie:

I was totally exhausted last night and fell asleep much before your Mom did. She woke me up as if the house was on fire, grabbed my hand and put it on her belly.

Now, I have this nasty little sleep-walking and talking habit. It rears its head at random times when I'll wake up messing around with ceiling tiles or asking my wife for scissors. So, jolting out of sleep to Jill grabbing my hand and putting it on her belly was a bit of a gamble on her part.

"You might be able to feel Donnie and Marie kick," she said. AND I DID! My eyes got really wide with excitement, and I wanted to say thank you. Both for the first kick and for the fact the house was not on fire.

Very exciting for me, funny how such a simple kick (or punch) can be so exciting.

Love,

Dad

The Dream

Tuesday September 12, 2006

Dear Donnie and Marie:

Of course, we don't know your gender. Kind of strange that it is written in a chart in the doctor's office, and THEY know, but we don't. It's not that we don't want to find out, because your Mom and I are absolutely dying to know, it's just that we think it will be the best possible gift to find out when you are born.

However, I had such an incredibly vivid dream last night... that you are a boy. I saw your wispy brown hair. You have your Mom's nose and chin and big hazel eyes. Have to tell you... you were pretty chunky as well, which is healthy.

We'll find out how close my dream was in a few short months, and we can't wait.

Love,

Dad

Your Parents Really Know How to Party

Thursday September 21, 2006

Dear Donnie and Marie:

Want to know how your parents roll on a Thursday night? A few years ago, the answer would've been a little different, but tonight we set up the music belt that I bought your Mom. We loaded speakers in the belt and plugged it into the CD player so that you could listen to some Mozart. We stopped shy of using the microphone to talk to you – figured you'll get plenty of our voices later!

We did listen though, since the kit also had a microphone that amplified your heartbeat and other noises. Didn't hear much except your Mom's giggling as we listened, but it was fun and bonding for us. No real furniture in your room except a crib, so we just camped out on the floor and listened to music along with you.

Whether or not the research proves to be correct that it stimulates your brain and improves mental development... it was a nice experience and we hope to do it some more... because we really know how to party.

Love,

Dad

Baby Stuff

Saturday October 15, 2006

Dear Donnie and Marie:

You are certainly on our minds a lot lately. Almost every conversation with a friend or family member revolves around you. And I don't know what you are building in what your cousin Carson calls a "baby house," but something weighs around 28 pounds right now.

According to a book we have, you are supposed to be around 2 pounds, and since Jill has put on 30 – you have created quite a little fortress for yourself in there. Pool table? Hot tub? What kind of mansion have you built already?

Your Grandma is coming in next weekend again, so we'll finish decorating your nursery. It's "reclining green," – thought you wouldn't mind. You have a great crib, seems nicer than your parents' bed.

The dresser turned out well and a reclining glider chair will be in there next week for you and Jill to hang out in. By the way, you'll have to let me know what you think of the music we have been playing for you. All classical, figured you can tune into hip hop a bit later in your life.

Last week you spent at the beach, playing in the water at St. George Island. This weekend you are getting pampered at the Ritz with a few other women. Basically, you're in a lap of luxury and you should be nice and relaxed for your debut in a couple months!

Next week, we're going to get another peek at you, an ultrasound. So get ready!

Love,

Dad

What's Your Name?

Thursday November 2, 2006

Dear Donnie and Marie:

We need to come up with a name for you! Or rather a couple names since we don't know if you are a boy or a girl. So as usual, when it comes to big decisions with your Mom, I put a lot of time into researching and thinking.

I looked up what names mean and thought about combinations of initials and nicknames, etc. Really don't want you to get beat up on the playground because your initials are WAD or something.

I wanted to go through my initial list once I had some really solid ideas and work them out with your Mom. Your Mom on the other hand was a fire hose of names/ideas non-stop. Just bouncing different variations of everything that came to her mind to see what might stick. Two very different approaches, but we pretty much are in agreement.

Sharing names before a baby is born is another thing people have very different opinions on. We chose not to share your name with anyone – which was my call. Your Mom of course wanted to tell everyone everything we are thinking. She gets to choose next time if we tell anyone or not.

My rationale is that it's our decision. Not anyone else's. So if someone else doesn't like the name, or used to date a stripper with that name – I don't really care. We wanted something that was not too common, but not so far out there that there will be a news story when you're born on your quack parents. Something that WE liked, not anyone else.

We may use the other name (for the other gender) if we decide to have a brother/sister for you, but this is what we are thinking...

If you are a boy, we like Samuel Lovett. Sam has a strong, simple, classic feel and while it has been popular in the past, it's not as common as other names today. Lovett of course is your Great-grandfather's last name. William (or Will) is one that was in the running for a long time – and who knows, we may decide you are a William in the end anyway!

If you are a girl we like Amelia Reese. Unique names we both love. We had a mutual friend in Chicago named Amelia and Reese is just a cool name – not really after the actress Reese Witherspoon, but we both like her also. One that we both really struggled with here is Katherine (Kate) – a name we both really like, but ended up going with our gut feeling and Amelia. Not easy decisions.

So there you go, a little insight into what your name might be – although the Donnie and Marie jokes will definitely live on!

Love,
Dad

---

33 Weeks

Sunday November 5, 2006

Dear Donnie and Marie:

"Kicking" doesn't really describe what you're doing now – it's more like you've invited some friends over and are thrashing in some sort of mash pit. Fun to feel, and thankfully your Mom thinks it's funny as well.

You got to stay up past your bed-time last night. We took you along on our date night to Dantanna's. Makes it cheaper without a babysitter.

Your Mom wasn't really sure what she wanted to eat, since you're giving her heartburn. I didn't have any problem deciding on surf & turf – I was really craving it. Then we took you along to a movie, which you seemed to sleep through.

We are both positive you are a boy, so it should be interesting to find out when December rolls around. Samantha Rose Weiner is here now, born a week or so ago, waiting for you to join a little play-group.

Of course, it's hilarious that there may be two Sams (different genders) across the street from each other, whose parents are friends! Oh well, we'll explain that one later.

Your Grandma came again last week, helped your Mom pick out a few more things and get set-up. Your room is basically done now – I think it looks nicer than our room – great colors, really luxurious crib and a nice glider chair for you and your Mom.

We've now taken infant CPR and "baby essentials" classes. Learned a few things, most important of which is that we (or I really) have no idea what to expect. Also learned that caffeine is absolutely critical for those classes – one of them your Mom asked me to leave because I was almost snoring.

Anyway, just thinking of you and wanted to jot you a quick note in-between working.

See you soon!

Love,

Dad

Show-time? When?

Saturday, December 09, 2006

Dear Donnie and Marie:

You're full term, which means you're big enough and healthy enough for show-time, as in a birth. So when is it going to be? I know your Mom is ready, since you've tacked on almost 50 pounds to her tiny frame that used to be around 100 pounds.

Her wrists hurt from ligaments separating, she downs Tums like candy, she has no idea where her feet are and is having trouble sleeping. She is way too positive to complain, but it is pretty obvious it's no fun. Your little kicks and flutters that used to make our eyes grow in excitement....now make our eyes grow in disbelief since we can see your foot coming out like an alien busting out of your Mom's belly.

We've toured the hospital, where I showcased my ignorance asking all kinds of questions I would've known the answers to if I read the stuff your Mom gave me. We took 10 more hours of birthing classes where we learned some relaxing techniques and a bunch of other stuff that we will hopefully remember for your big show. All this to go toward my Master's degree in "I don't have a clue."

Your Mom has the car seat all ready to go and your nursery has everything except a big-screen TV and disco ball.

So, again, when's it going to be? Your Mom's last appointment revealed you descended, which was easy to see for ourselves – since you and your 50-pound dance party are visibly lower on your Mom.

Now we are just waiting. I have a special cell phone that is the "I'm going into labor" phone. I keep it as close to my skin as possible so I can feel it vibrate if I can't hear the ring.

We'll keep talking to you, playing you music and wondering…whenever you're ready…come out here! It's more fun.

Love you,

Dad

Tumble

Saturday, December 16, 2006

Dear Donnie and Marie:

In my current job, I tend to have 3 or 4 cell phones in my pockets at any given time. Yesterday, the special phone, with a special ring… rang. It's the one that is dedicated to your Mom calling when you're on the way. So you can imagine how I jumped out of my skin while I was on a conference call.

It was not the news I was hoping for.

Your Mom said, "I'm OK, but I just fell down the stairs."

I raced home and we spend 4.5 hours in the hospital last night, just listening to and watching the monitor of your heart beat. Not fun, but you appear to be OK. Your Mom is OK, just rattled, and can't say I had much fun.

It is time for you to get on this side of the world, we are ready and the anticipation is really building. We know it will be a memorable holiday season, we just don't know which day to celebrate yet! How about this tax year?

Love,

Dad

Christmas

Saturday, December 23, 2006

Dear Donnie and Marie:

When I was younger, say 4 or 5 years old… the anticipation of Christmas was intense. It was such a long month of December, waiting each day until Santa came.

When I was a bit older, say 9 or 10, the anticipation got even worse – a buzzing sound that started right after Thanksgiving. I would shoot out of bed each morning and run to open another day of the advent calendar, wondering if I could speed the process somehow if I opened the next two days.

Now I'm 32 years old. It's fun to see the looks on other people's faces when they get their gifts. Actually, it's fun to see the looks even if they hate their gifts.

"Oh, that's… greeeaat, thank you SO much, I really was thinking about getting a rooster timer for the kitchen…" Christmas snuck up on me again this year. I mean, it's in two days. Not that I didn't know it was coming, it's just the hype of malls, movies, caroling... kind of passed me over.

However, the anticipation of your birth is driving me crazy! It's just like when I was 9 or 10 years old – when will Donnie and Marie come?

Today? On Wednesday of last week your Mom's appointment revealed she was dilated 1 centimeter. So that's progress, but really no indication of when you're going to show up. Maybe this afternoon… maybe your due date on the 27th? The doctor said they would induce on the 28th (incidentally predicted to be the highest day of births of the year – for the tax break and to not cramp hospital's New Year's plans I guess).

There were memorable Christmas holidays as a boy and many that have quite honestly run together. Maybe that makes me sound Scrooge-like, but my point is that this Christmas is already memorable – since you are on the way. And given the way your Mom is hobbling around, you may be coming out with a sleigh and a couple tiny reindeer. Get out of her belly and come give me a hug!

Love,

Dad

Finally, the Beginning

Saturday, January 6, 2007

Dear Donnie and Marie:

The last week has been a blur, but you are here! You were due December 27th – which came and went. We were planning to go in to the hospital so that your Mom could be induced that evening, but the hospital was full. Last Thursday was December 28th, and we were going to try again to go in the hospital in the evening, but we weren't sure of our chances – lots of inductions at the end of the year for a variety of reasons.

Then we got the call.

At noon on the 28th, we drove to Northside Hospital, not entirely sure what to expect – despite all the classes we took and books "we" read. They gave your Mom a treatment to slowly induce labor. Slowly is right.

The contractions started getting pretty bad at 3am on Friday morning, the 29th. She was 3 centimeters dilated by that point and wanted an epidural. The next 9 hours were completely restless for me, camping out on the hospital room couch and obviously not much better for your Mom, even with an epidural.

She was hooked up to a monitor for your heart rate and one for contractions and every time she needed to get up, I unhooked all the cords and hooked them back up.

Plenty of coffee and McDonalds later (the only place to eat when I was hungry), the nurses came in and said, "Let's try to push a little." That was at 11:45 am on Friday the 29th. Your Mom was completely dilated and they were just testing the waters to see what was going to happen. Well, you started flying out.

The nurse showed me your head – a smattering of black hair. I had a couple duties here: 1) not pass out, 2) announce the gender, and 3) cut the umbilical cord. Your Mom had one duty – get you out!

The midwife came in, told me to grab a leg and your Mom pushed. Now, what's interesting about this is that I had absolutely no intentions of grabbing a leg going in. I mistakenly thought that I would be hanging out near your Mom's head, while something was going on down there. Somehow, it didn't cross my mind that Jill is a little over five feet tall, so scrunched up there really isn't that much room between her head and "down there." Needless to say, when the midwife told me to grab a leg, I just grabbed a leg. I did however, position a chair behind me just in case I failed at my job #1 (not passing out).

In 15 minutes and 5 pushes – you were out! I put my glasses on before the last push just so I could make sure I got the gender right – you are a boy!!!

6 pounds 15 ounces, 20 inches long. Blackish hair, blue eyes (for now) and not really sure who you look like yet.

I cut the cord, and you got all dried off. Your Mom was an absolute champion.

I couldn't wait to share pictures – 10s of thousands of hits to the site where I posted them at this point.

So, you were poked and prodded over the next week and after 4 days, 3 nights in the hospital we could come home. Your Mom is doing great, although the new "sleep" schedule is tough. But now we finally have the beginning.

We love you and have never been so happy to have something that is normal (and handsome) – even when you're peeing on my leg.

Love,

Dad

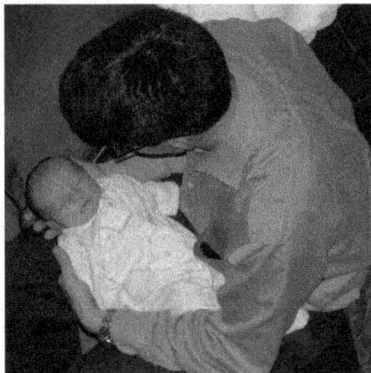

Almost a Year

Thursday December 27, 2007

Dear Sam Hammer:

People say it all the time, but it really is hard to believe almost a year has gone by. We have wonderful pictures from the last 12 months trying to do justice to the ball of fun and fury you are – a whole year of firsts.

Your first Mother's and Father's Day, your first trip out of the state, your first Halloween and first Christmas...and in two days your first birthday. Essentially, we have pictures of a whole pile of firsts that were really more interesting for us than for you.

We also have a year full of movies that I'll edit into a few minutes that we can tolerate to watch – minus the screeching cooing of (names withheld intentionally).

A few of my 2007 highlights included your first real smiles around 2-3 months old. Giggling came pretty soon afterward, which is just priceless. Of course, now when your giggle box turns over it's hard for you to stand up, which is hilarious.

Somewhere around 6-7 months I think you figured out that I was more than a "not-Mommy," but am actually a "Daddy." Now that you are 12 months old, you definitely know your Daddy, so good progress there.

I definitely remember the first couple times you were cleared for take-off on aircraft carrier "The Daddy." Pure joy on your crazy mostly-toothless, vampire smile.

You took your first legitimate steps and were walking at 8 months-old. Pretty proud that you had little interest in crawling and just sprung up and started a series of Samclones (whirring and spinning everything off whatever is in reach).

In the next year, I'm looking forward to playing ball with you. Right now you're curious about playing ball – bouncing them, tossing them and kicking them, but it's still more interesting to see what things taste like than tossing a ball with your old man. We'll soon fix that!

Happy random Thursday young man. I look forward to many more with you – since we are pals.

Love,

Dad

First B-day

Dear Sam Man:

OK pal, you're officially a year old today! Time to share a few pics:

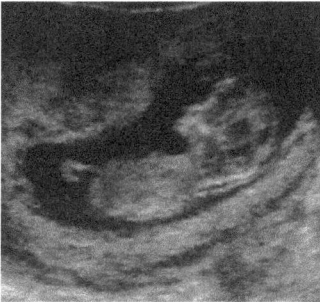

6.06

11.06

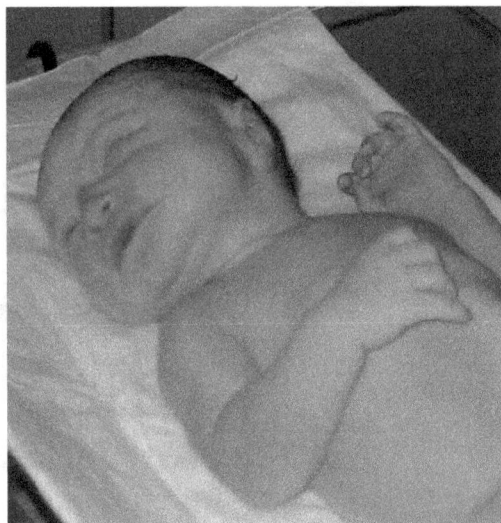

12.29.06

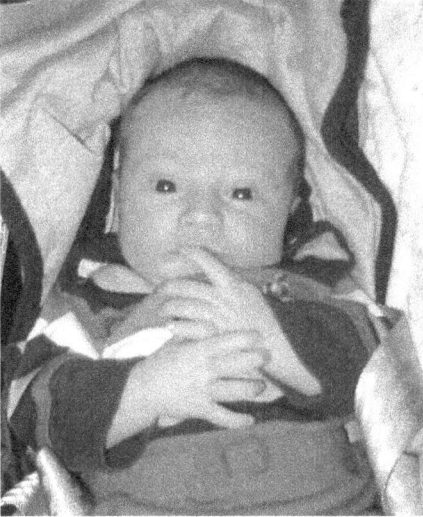

1.07

3.07

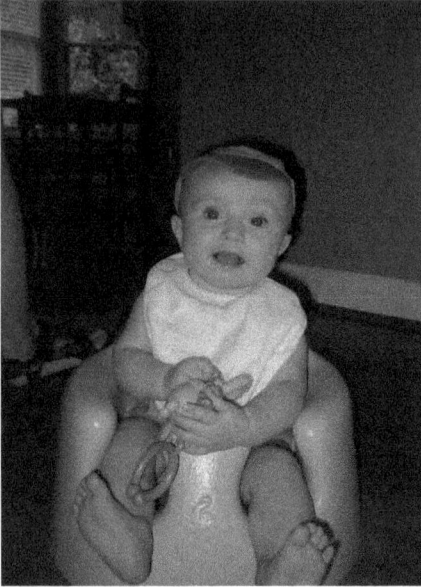

6.07

7.07

8.07

10.07

10.07

10.07

10.07

12.07

12.07

12.07

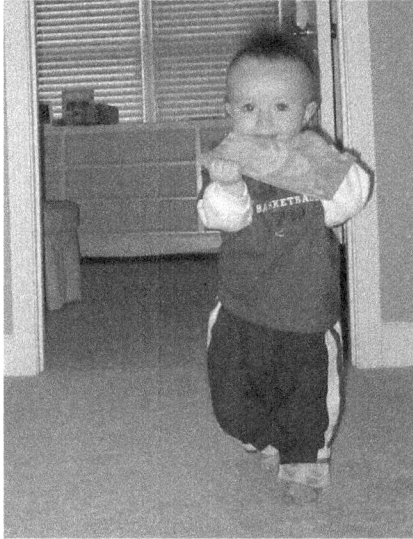

12.29.07

Your birthday party is over and you have more gifts than you know what to do with – not to mention the hours of fun with the boxes. In typical fashion for your Mom, what started out as a few family members coming over turned into 25 people + a pile of kids.

Truthfully, she did a nice job hosting. Nice snacks and contained chaos. And you were a champion with only one meltdown. We sang happy birthday, you smeared your face with icing, then the long dramatic pause as the whole house watched your next move was enough to start the tears. It was fun overall, with some great pictures to prove it.

So that's a wrap – one year, one volume of letters. Certainly there will be more firsts next year, with more reasons to write you. Maybe a first word is around the corner? Or the first time your hair won't stick straight up off your head?

Thank you Sam, for the reason to do this.

Love,

Dad

www.ingramcontent.com/pod-product-compliance
Lightning Source LLC
Chambersburg PA
CBHW030305030426
42337CB00012B/587